Think Less, Live More: Break Free from Overthinking

This book offers clear, actionable steps for the you to move from overthinking to living a more peaceful, stress-free life.

PUBLISHED BY: Ashwanee Gupta

Ashwanee Gupta

Copyright © 2024 All rights reserved.

No part of this publication may be copied, reproduced in any format, by any means, electronic or otherwise, without prior consent from the copyright owner and publisher of this book.

Think Less, Live More

The Journey Ahead

Overcoming overthinking isn't an overnight fix. It's a journey, a process that requires patience, practice, and consistency. But rest assured, with each step you take, you'll find that the mental clutter will begin to clear. Your thoughts will become more focused, your stress will begin to melt away, and you'll feel more grounded and connected to the present moment.

The steps outlined in the chapters ahead will guide you to release the weight of overthinking, so you can start living a life that feels lighter, more alive, and full of peace. It's time to begin your journey from overthinking to living more fully.

Let's get started.

Table of Contents:

Introduction: Understanding Overthinking and Its Impact

Overthinking is a modern epidemic. In today's fast-paced world, with endless distractions and constant pressure to do more, be more, and achieve more, it's no surprise that overthinking has become a default state for many. But while it feels like a natural response to life's challenges, overthinking can trap us in a cycle of stress, anxiety, and wasted time, ultimately preventing us from living a meaningful, peaceful life.

In this book, we will explore what overthinking is, how it impacts every aspect of your life, and, most importantly, how you can break free from it. By following the simple yet powerful steps you'll learn to take control of your thoughts, minimize stress, and cultivate a life that is more peaceful, more focused, and ultimately more fulfilling.

This journey isn't about changing who you are. It's about unlocking the power that's already within you—power that has been buried beneath layers of anxiety, worry, and endless mental chatter. Once you break free from the overthinking trap, you'll rediscover a sense of freedom and clarity that will allow you to live life more fully and with greater joy.

The Silent Struggle of Overthinking

Overthinking is often an invisible burden. Unlike physical ailments, it doesn't have a visible, tangible symptom that you can point to. It doesn't require a doctor's visit or a prescription. Instead, it's the constant chatter in your mind—the worry about what might happen, what could go wrong, or how you could have done things differently. Overthinking is a sneaky, silent thief that robs you of time and peace without you even realizing it.

Overthinkers tend to replay scenarios over and over again, imagining all the possible outcomes, no matter how far-fetched or unrealistic. They mentally rehearse conversations that haven't happened yet, or dissect events from the past with a microscope, attempting to pinpoint every small mistake or flaw. This cycle leaves them feeling mentally exhausted, anxious, and often paralyzed by indecision.

For some, this constant mental chatter can lead to feelings of inadequacy, fear of making the wrong choice, or a sense of being overwhelmed. It can become so pervasive that it starts to impact their relationships, productivity, and overall sense of well-being.

The True Cost of Overthinking

At first glance, overthinking may seem like a harmless habit. After all, thinking deeply about a problem is usually a sign of intelligence and concern, right? But when thinking spirals out of control, it becomes a problem. The real cost of overthinking is much higher than most realize.

Overthinking naturally leads to increased levels of stress and anxiety. When we obsess over a situation, we're essentially rehearsing all possible negative outcomes in our minds, which feeds into worry and uncertainty. This constant stress can harm your mental and physical health, leading to insomnia, headaches, fatigue, and digestive issues.

Instead of focusing on productive action, overthinking steals valuable time. You may find yourself stuck in a loop of thoughts, wasting precious hours on scenarios that might never even happen. Over time, this leads to procrastination, missed opportunities, and a general feeling of being "stuck."

Overthinking often leads to decision-making paralysis. When faced with a choice, you may overanalyze every option until you feel completely frozen, unable to make a decision. This causes unnecessary delays and prevents you from taking action, which only feeds into the cycle of overthinking.

Overthinking doesn't just affect you—it affects those around you. Constant worry or overanalyzing situations can cause misunderstandings, miscommunications, and tension in relationships. Friends, family, and colleagues may not understand why you are so distracted or hesitant, leading to frustration on both sides.

The Science Behind Overthinking

Understanding the science behind overthinking can be a crucial step in breaking free from its grip. The brain is wired to solve problems, which is why overthinking can feel like a natural response when we're facing challenges. But when overthinking becomes habitual, it starts to work against us.

The prefrontal cortex, the part of the brain responsible for higher-level thinking, decision-making, and problem-solving, is where overthinking originates. It's designed to help us make sense of situations and plan for the future. However, when this part of the brain is overwhelmed by excessive information or emotions, it can get stuck in a loop of rumination.

Overthinking often triggers the body's fight-or-flight response, even when there's no immediate danger. When we're caught in a mental loop, our body can experience the physical symptoms of stress—such as a racing heart, shallow breathing, and muscle tension—despite being in a safe environment. This reaction further fuels the cycle of anxiety and overthinking.

Overthinking is self-reinforcing. The more we overthink, the more stress and anxiety we feel, which leads to more overthinking. The cycle continues, sometimes escalating, until it becomes almost impossible to break free.

The Path to Freedom: What This Book Will Do for You

In "Think Less, Live More," the goal is simple: to help you break the cycle of overthinking and transform your mental landscape into a space of calm, focus, and clarity. The book is designed to give you both the understanding and the practical tools you need to change your relationship with your thoughts.

What you will learn:

- How to recognize and interrupt the patterns of overthinking.

- Effective techniques to reduce stress and quiet your mind.

- Practical steps to take control of your thoughts, instead of letting them control you.

- How to cultivate mental clarity and peace, even in the midst of challenges.

- Simple, actionable habits that will make calmness and focus your new default state.

By the end of this book, you'll not only have the tools to manage your overthinking but also gain a deeper understanding of yourself and your mind. You will have the power to think less, live more, and achieve a life filled with peace, purpose, and joy.

By the end of this book, you'll not only have the tools to manage your overthinking but also gain a deeper understanding of yourself and your mind. You will have the power to think less, live more, and achieve a life filled with peace, purpose, and joy.

Chapter 1:

Awareness – Recognizing Overthinking Patterns

Overthinking is like a rocking chair—it gives you something to do but gets you nowhere. It keeps your mind stuck, replaying past mistakes, worrying about the future, or obsessing over trivial details. But here's the truth: until you become aware of it, you can't break free from it. This chapter is your first step to understanding how overthinking operates and how to spot its patterns in your life.

1.1: What Overthinking Looks Like

Imagine a boy named Sam. Sam is a bright student, but every time he finishes an assignment, he spends hours agonizing over whether it's good enough. "Did I answer that question correctly? What if the teacher thinks it's sloppy? Maybe I should redo it," he tells himself. By the end of the night, Sam has rewritten his assignment three times and is still not satisfied.

This is overthinking—a relentless cycle of mental gymnastics that leads to stress, fatigue, and wasted time. Overthinking doesn't always look like Sam's story. For some, it's lying awake at night replaying a conversation, wondering if you said the wrong thing. For others, it's an endless search for the "perfect" decision, whether it's what to wear, what to eat, or which job to take.

"Don't get stuck in the paralysis of analysis." – Tony Robbins

Overthinking tricks us into believing we're being productive, but in reality, we're just running in circles. Recognizing when and how you overthink is the first step to breaking free from its grip.

1.2: The Cost of Overthinking

Let's meet Sarah, a 35-year-old marketing manager. Sarah was offered a promotion at work. Instead of celebrating, she spent weeks overanalyzing every aspect of the new role. "What if I'm not good enough? What if my coworkers resent me? What if I fail?" These thoughts consumed her so much that she declined the promotion, fearing she couldn't handle the pressure.

This is the hidden cost of overthinking: it steals your opportunities, time, and peace of mind. Studies show that chronic overthinkers are more likely to experience anxiety, depression, and burnout. It's like carrying a backpack filled with rocks everywhere you go—you may not notice it at first, but over time, it weighs you down.

Key Takeaways:

1. Overthinking creates self-doubt and hesitation.

2. It drains your energy and limits your potential.

3. It prevents you from enjoying the present moment.

1.3: The Power of Awareness

A man was walking through a forest when he accidentally stepped on a thorn. Instead of removing the thorn, he sat down and began to obsess over why it had happened. "Why didn't I see it? What's wrong with me? Should I have taken another path?" Hours passed, and the thorn remained stuck in his foot, causing pain and infection.

This story illustrates the power of awareness. The moment you recognize that you're caught in an overthinking spiral, you can stop, take action, and remove the "thorn." Awareness is like a flashlight in a dark room—it helps you see the clutter in your mind so you can start clearing it out.

Exercise:

Try the "Thought Log" technique. For one week, keep a small notebook with you and jot down any repetitive or anxious thoughts. At the end of each day, review your list. You'll start noticing patterns, like certain triggers or recurring themes. Awareness begins with observation.

"You can't fix what you don't acknowledge." – Dr. Phil

1.4: Breaking the Habit of Overthinking

Awareness is the foundation, but breaking the habit requires action. Start small:

1. Set time limits for decision-making. For example, give yourself 10 minutes to decide what to eat for dinner or 30 minutes to draft an email.

2. Shift your focus. When you catch yourself overthinking, redirect your attention to a physical activity, like stretching, walking, or deep breathing.

3. Challenge your thoughts. Ask yourself, "Is this thought helpful or harmful?" and "What's the worst that could happen?"

Let's go back to Sam. After learning to recognize his overthinking, he started setting time limits for assignments. He realized his first draft was usually good enough, and he used the extra time to relax and pursue hobbies he enjoyed.

Conclusion

Overthinking isn't a problem you solve overnight, but awareness is the first step on your journey. Like a traffic light, it tells you when to stop, look around, and decide on a new direction. By identifying your overthinking patterns, understanding their cost, and practicing awareness, you lay the groundwork for a calmer, more focused mind.

Questions:

1. Can you recall a recent situation where you overthought something? What was the outcome?

2. What triggers your overthinking? Is it fear of failure, perfectionism, or something else?

3. How can you use the "Thought Log" technique to gain more clarity?

Chapter 2:

Mindfulness – Grounding Yourself in the Present

Overthinking often takes us on a mental time-travel adventure, dragging us into the past or flinging us into the future. The problem? We miss out on the only moment that truly matters: the present. Mindfulness is the antidote—a powerful tool that anchors us in the here and now. This chapter will introduce you to mindfulness and teach you how to use it to quiet your mind and reclaim your peace.

2.1: What Is Mindfulness?

Imagine this: You're eating your favorite ice cream, but instead of savoring the creamy sweetness, your mind is racing. Did I send that email? What if I said the wrong thing in the meeting? Oh no, I forgot to pay that bill. The ice cream melts away, unnoticed, as your thoughts spiral.

Mindfulness is the opposite of this mental chaos. It's about fully experiencing the present moment—tasting that ice cream, feeling the coldness on your tongue, and enjoying the simple pleasure without distractions.

Jon Kabat-Zinn, often called the father of modern mindfulness, defines it as "paying attention in a particular way: on purpose, in the present moment, and nonjudgmentally." Mindfulness isn't about clearing your mind or forcing yourself to think positively. It's about noticing your thoughts without judgment and gently bringing your focus back to the now.

"Mindfulness is a way of befriending ourselves and our experience." – Jon Kabat-Zinn

2.2: Why Mindfulness Works for Overthinking

Let's meet Emily. Emily is a college student who often gets stuck in "what if" scenarios. Before every test, she thinks, What if I fail? What if I studied the wrong material? What if everyone else does better than me? Her anxiety spirals until she can't concentrate.

Emily discovered mindfulness during a stress management workshop. The instructor taught her to focus on her breath whenever she felt overwhelmed. Instead of getting lost in her thoughts, she learned to observe them like passing clouds. Over time, she realized that her thoughts didn't control her— she could let them go.

Mindfulness works because it disrupts the overthinking loop. When you're fully present, your brain has no room for worries about the past or future. Instead, it focuses on what's real and immediate.

Key Benefits of Mindfulness:

1. Reduces stress and anxiety by calming the mind.

2. Improves focus and concentration.

3. Helps you respond to situations instead of reacting impulsively.

2.3: Simple Mindfulness Practices

Mindfulness doesn't require hours of meditation or a special retreat. It's something you can practice anywhere, anytime. Let's explore a few simple techniques:

1. The 5-4-3-2-1 Grounding Exercise

This exercise brings your attention to the present moment by engaging your senses.

- Name 5 things you can see.

- Name 4 things you can touch.

- Name 3 things you can hear.

- Name 2 things you can smell.

- Name 1 thing you can taste.

This technique is perfect for calming your mind during moments of stress or overthinking.

2. Mindful Breathing

Take a moment to sit quietly and focus on your breath. Notice the sensation of air entering your nose and filling your lungs. If your mind wanders, gently bring it back to your breath. Start with just one minute and gradually increase the time.

3. Mindful Eating

The next time you eat, slow down. Notice the colors, textures, and flavors of your food. Chew slowly and savor each bite. Not only does this practice reduce mindless eating, but it also helps you appreciate the present moment.

2.4: Staying Present When the Mind Wanders

Even with practice, your mind will wander—that's natural. The goal of mindfulness isn't to stop wandering thoughts but to notice them and bring your attention back to the present.

A monk was once asked, "What do you gain from meditation?" He replied, "I gain nothing. But I lose anger, anxiety, and insecurity."

Mindfulness isn't about perfection. It's about progress. Every time you catch your mind wandering and bring it back to the present, you're strengthening your mental muscles, just like lifting weights at the gym.

When you notice overthinking creeping in, try saying to yourself, "Right now, I'm okay." This simple affirmation helps ground you in the present moment and reminds you that most of your worries exist only in your mind.

"Do not dwell in the past, do not dream of the future, concentrate the mind on the present moment." – Buddha

2.5: How to Make Mindfulness a Daily Habit

Habits are the building blocks of change. To make mindfulness a part of your life, start small and be consistent.

- Choose a specific time each day—like when you wake up or before bedtime—to practice mindfulness. Even five minutes a day can make a difference.
- Apps like Headspace or Calm offer guided meditations and mindfulness exercises to keep you on track.
- You can practice mindfulness while brushing your teeth, washing dishes, or walking. The key is to focus fully on the activity and let go of distracting thoughts.

David, a busy entrepreneur, used to think he had no time for mindfulness. But he started practicing mindful walking during his daily commute. Instead of scrolling through his phone, he focused on the rhythm of his steps and the sights and sounds around him. This simple shift transformed his mornings, making him feel more grounded and less stressed.

Conclusion

Mindfulness isn't just a practice—it's a way of life. By learning to stay present, you can escape the endless loops of overthinking and find clarity in the chaos. Whether it's through mindful breathing, eating, or walking, these small, intentional moments help you reconnect with yourself and the world around you.

Reflection Questions:

1. What activity could you turn into a mindful practice this week?

2. How do you feel after trying one of the mindfulness exercises?

3. What distracts you most from staying present, and how can you address it?

As you embrace mindfulness, you'll discover that the present moment is not only enough—it's everything.

Chapter 3:

Reframing Negative Thoughts – Shifting Your Mindset

Our thoughts shape our reality. Negative thinking, often fueled by overthinking, can create a cycle of doubt, fear, and self-criticism. But here's the good news: you have the power to change your perspective. This chapter focuses on the art of reframing negative thoughts and transforming your mindset from one of limitation to one of possibility.

3.1: The Power of Perspective

A traveler came across two stonecutters working on a cathedral. He asked the first stonecutter what he was doing. "I'm cutting stones to earn a living," the man replied. When the traveler asked the second stonecutter the same question, he smiled and said, "I'm building a magnificent cathedral that will inspire generations."

Both men were performing the same task, but their perspectives couldn't have been more different. This story illustrates the power of reframing—choosing to see a situation in a more empowering light.

Negative thoughts often distort our perspective. They magnify failures, minimize achievements, and paint worst-case scenarios. Reframing helps you see the bigger picture and reinterpret challenges as opportunities for growth.

"Whether you think you can, or you think you can't—you're right." – Henry Ford

3.2: Recognizing Cognitive Distortions

Before you can reframe a negative thought, you need to recognize it. Negative thinking often takes the form of cognitive distortions—automatic, irrational thought patterns.

Here are some common ones:

1. Catastrophizing: Expecting the worst-case scenario.

   o Example: "If I make a mistake at work, I'll get fired."

2. Black-and-White Thinking: Viewing things as all good or all bad.

   o Example: "If I don't succeed, I'm a total failure."

3. Mind Reading: Assuming you know what others are thinking.

   o Example: "They didn't respond to my text, so they must be mad at me."

Takeaway:
Cognitive distortions fuel overthinking and negativity. By identifying them, you can begin to challenge and change them.

3.3: Techniques for Reframing Thoughts

Reframing is like putting on a new pair of glasses—it changes how you see the world. Let's explore some techniques to help you do this:

1. **Ask Better Questions**

   When faced with a negative thought, ask yourself:
   - "Is this thought true?"
   - "What evidence do I have for and against it?"
   - "What's a more realistic way to view this situation?"

2. **Turn "What If" into "Even If"** Instead of worrying, What if things go wrong? try thinking, Even if things don't go as planned, I can handle it.

Rachel, a young artist, was terrified of sharing her work because she thought, What if people don't like it? Her mentor encouraged her to reframe her fear: Even if some people don't like it, others might love it. And either way, it's an opportunity to learn and grow. This shift gave Rachel the courage to display her art, which was met with overwhelming praise.

3. **Practice Gratitude**

   Gratitude helps you focus on what's good in your life rather than what's lacking. Start each day by listing three things you're grateful for. This simple practice trains your brain to notice the positive.

3.4: The Role of Self-Talk

Negative thoughts often manifest as harsh self-talk. You might catch yourself thinking, *I'm so stupid* or *I'll never succeed.* Imagine saying those words to a close friend—you wouldn't! So why say them to yourself?

"Talk to yourself like you would to someone you love." – Brené Brown

To change your self-talk:

1. Catch It: Notice when you're being self-critical.

2. Challenge It: Ask, "Would I say this to a friend?"

3. Change It: Replace harsh words with kinder, more supportive ones.

Example:
Instead of thinking, *I'm terrible at this,* try, *I'm still learning, and that's okay.*

3.5: Transforming Setbacks into Stepping Stones

Reframing isn't just about shifting your mindset in small moments—it's also about viewing challenges as opportunities.

Thomas Edison failed thousands of times before inventing the light bulb. When asked about his failures, he famously said, "I have not failed. I've just found 10,000 ways that won't work." Edison's ability to reframe setbacks as learning experiences is a powerful reminder that failure is not the opposite of success—it's part of the journey.

The next time you face a setback, write down:

1. What went wrong.

2. What you learned from the experience.

3. How you can use this knowledge moving forward.

3.6: Building a Reframing Habit

Changing your mindset takes practice, but it's worth the effort. Here's how to make reframing a habit:

1. Keep a Thought Journal: Write down negative thoughts and how you reframe them. Over time, this will strengthen your ability to think positively.

2. Surround Yourself with Positivity: Spend time with people who uplift you and inspire you to see the best in situations.

3. **Celebrate Small Wins:** Acknowledge and reward yourself every time you successfully reframe a negative thought.

Conclusion

Reframing negative thoughts isn't about ignoring problems or pretending everything is perfect. It's about choosing a perspective that empowers you rather than limits you. By recognizing cognitive distortions, practicing gratitude, and changing your self-talk, you can transform your mindset and break free from the cycle of negativity.

Reflection Questions:

1. What negative thought have you been holding onto, and how can you reframe it?

2. Which cognitive distortion do you recognize in yourself most often?

3. How can you start practicing gratitude in your daily life?

Chapter 4:

Time Management – Taking Control of Your Day

Overthinking often hijacks our time, leaving us overwhelmed and unproductive. This chapter focuses on practical strategies to reclaim your day, reduce mental clutter, and achieve more with less stress.

4.1: The Time-Thinking Connection

Overthinking doesn't just drain mental energy; it also wastes precious time. When you're stuck in indecision or replaying scenarios, you're robbed of the opportunity to take meaningful action.

Ethan, a college student, spent hours debating whether to start a project or wait for "inspiration." By the time he finally started, he was rushed and stressed, realizing he had wasted hours in analysis paralysis.

Key Insights:

- **The Paradox of Productivity: The more you overthink, the less you accomplish.**

- **Identifying Time Traps: Common pitfalls like procrastination, perfectionism, and multitasking often stem from overthinking.**

Exercise:
Write down how much time you spend thinking about tasks instead of doing them. Reflect on what could be achieved if that energy was redirected to action.

"You may delay, but time will not." – Benjamin Franklin

4.2: Prioritization – Separating What Matters from the Noise

Effective time management begins with understanding what truly matters. Overthinkers often give equal weight to all tasks, leading to overwhelm.

Techniques to Master Prioritization:

1. **The Eisenhower Matrix: Categorize tasks into:**

   o **Urgent and important: Do these immediately.**

   o **Important but not urgent: Schedule these.**

   o **Urgent but not important: Delegate or minimize these.**

   o **Neither urgent nor important: Eliminate these.**

Example:
A working mom used the Eisenhower Matrix to delegate house

chores and focus on her business goals, reducing stress and boosting productivity.

2. The 80/20 Rule: Focus on the 20% of tasks that yield 80% of results.

Jessica, a marketing professional, identified her most impactful work was in client presentations. By prioritizing this, she doubled her productivity while working fewer hours.

Exercise:
List your tasks for the day. Assign each one to an Eisenhower Matrix quadrant, and act accordingly.

Subchapter 4.3: Structuring Your Day for Success

A structured day minimizes decision fatigue and overthinking. Creating routines and habits frees your mind for higher-level thinking and reduces stress.

Steps to Build a Routine:

1. Morning Routine: Start with intentional actions like meditation, journaling, or exercise to set the tone for the day.

2. Time Blocking: Assign specific hours for focused work, breaks, and relaxation.

3. Evening Reflection: Review your accomplishments and plan for the next day.

Liam, a freelance designer, used to work sporadically and felt constantly behind. After implementing time blocking, he found he could finish his projects ahead of schedule and had more free time.

Tips for Sticking to a Schedule:

- Use a planner or digital calendar.

- Set reminders to keep yourself on track.

- Reward yourself for sticking to your plan.

"Either you run the day, or the day runs you." – Jim Rohn

Exercise:
Plan tomorrow using a time-blocking method. Include work, breaks, and personal time. Stick to it for one day and observe the impact.

Conclusion to Chapter 4

Time is one of our most valuable resources, and overthinking is its greatest thief. By understanding the connection between overthinking and time loss, prioritizing effectively, and structuring your day, you can take back control and accomplish more with ease.

Reflection Questions:

1. How much time do you spend on overthinking instead of doing?

2. What is one task you can eliminate or delegate today?

3. How can you create a routine that reduces decision fatigue?

Think Less, Live More

Chapter 5:

Practicing Self-Compassion – Silencing the Inner Critic

Overthinking often feeds on self-criticism and unrealistic expectations. The antidote? Self-compassion. By treating yourself with the kindness you would show a friend, you can quiet the harsh inner critic and build a healthier, more forgiving relationship with yourself. This chapter explores the transformative power of self-compassion and how it can free you from the cycle of overthinking.

5.1: Understanding Self-Compassion

Self-compassion is the practice of being kind to yourself, especially in moments of failure or difficulty. It involves three key elements:

1. **Self-Kindness:** Replacing self-judgment with understanding.

2. **Common Humanity:** Recognizing that everyone makes mistakes.

3. **Mindfulness:** Acknowledging your emotions without being overwhelmed by them.

"Talk to yourself like someone you love." – Brené Brown

Example:
If you make a mistake at work, instead of berating yourself, self-compassion helps you think: *"Mistakes happen. What can I learn from this?"*

5.2: The Role of Self-Criticism in Overthinking

Overthinking often stems from self-doubt and perfectionism. Thoughts like *"Why did I say that?"* or *"What if I fail?"* create a loop of negativity. Self-compassion breaks this loop by offering an alternative narrative—one rooted in understanding and growth.

Amy, a high school student, struggled with overthinking after failing a math test. Her inner critic kept repeating, *"You're not smart enough."* After learning about self-compassion, she started telling herself, *"Everyone has bad days. I'll study differently next time."* This shift helped her focus on solutions instead of self-blame.

5.3: Overcoming Barriers to Self-Compassion

Practicing self-compassion can feel awkward or unnatural, especially if you're used to being hard on yourself.

Common Challenges:

- **Feeling unworthy of kindness.**

- **Fearing it will make you less motivated.**

Tip:
Remember, self-compassion fuels motivation. When you're kind to yourself, you're more likely to bounce back from setbacks.

"No one can make you feel inferior without your consent." –
Eleanor Roosevelt

5.4: The Long-Term Benefits of Self-Compassion

Over time, self-compassion rewires your brain to be less reactive and more resilient.

Key Benefits:

- **Reduces overthinking and self-doubt.**

- **Enhances emotional regulation.**

- **Improves relationships by reducing defensiveness and increasing empathy.**

Mark, a perfectionist, used self-compassion to stop overanalyzing his mistakes. He found that being kind to himself actually improved his performance at work and strengthened his friendships.

5.5: Self-Compassion in Everyday Life

Incorporate self-compassion into your routine:

- **Morning Mantra:** Start your day with a kind statement like, *"I'm doing my best, and that's enough."*

- **Pause and Reflect:** When you feel overwhelmed, take a moment to breathe and remind yourself, *"It's okay to not have everything figured out."*

Example:
During her morning coffee, Lily spent two minutes repeating a self-compassionate affirmation. This small habit set a positive tone for her entire day.

Conclusion

Self-compassion is a cornerstone of overcoming overthinking. By treating yourself with kindness and understanding, you dismantle the inner critic and create space for growth and peace.

Reflection Questions:

1. What's one area of your life where you can be kinder to yourself?

2. How would your inner dialogue change if you treated yourself like a friend?

3. What's one self-compassion exercise you can try today?

Chapter 6:

Decluttering the Mind – Clearing Mental Clutter for Inner Peace

Just as a cluttered desk can hinder productivity, a cluttered mind can overwhelm and exhaust us. Mental clutter—unresolved thoughts, unaddressed worries, and unnecessary distractions—fuels overthinking and drains our emotional energy. In this chapter, we'll uncover practical strategies to declutter your mind, allowing you to focus on what truly matters and find peace amidst the chaos.

6.1: What Is Mental Clutter?

Mental clutter can take many forms:

- Worries about the future.

- Regrets about the past.

- Endless to-do lists.

- Constant notifications and information overload.

Jake was a young professional juggling work, relationships, and personal goals. His mind constantly raced with thoughts like, *Did I forget to send that email?* or *What if I said the wrong thing in yesterday's meeting?* One day, he realized his mental clutter was preventing him from enjoying the present. Determined to change, Jake began organizing his thoughts the same way he'd declutter a messy room—one step at a time.

6.2: The Hidden Costs of Mental Clutter

Carrying too much mental clutter can:

- Increase stress and anxiety.

- Impair decision-making.

- Distract you from meaningful moments.

"You can't pour from an empty cup. Take care of yourself first." – Unknown

Mental decluttering isn't a luxury; it's a necessity for maintaining balance and clarity in your life.

6.3: Step 1 – Brain Dump: Get It All Out

A brain dump is a simple yet powerful exercise:

1. Take a pen and paper (or a digital tool).

2. Write down every thought, worry, or task occupying your mind.

3. **Don't organize—just let it flow.**

Writing down your thoughts clears your mind, giving you space to prioritize and focus.

Example:
Emily, a college student, felt overwhelmed by upcoming exams and personal commitments. After doing a brain dump, she realized that half of her worries were minor tasks she could delegate or schedule later. The exercise immediately made her feel lighter.

6.4: Step 2 – Prioritize What Matters

Not everything on your mental list deserves equal attention. Use tools like:

- The Eisenhower Matrix: Categorize tasks into urgent, important, and non-essential.

- The 80/20 Rule: Focus on the 20% of tasks that yield 80% of results.

Raj, a startup founder, constantly felt overwhelmed by decisions. After prioritizing tasks using the 80/20 rule, he discovered that focusing on customer feedback (20%) drove most of his company's growth (80%).

6.5: Step 3 – Let Go of What You Can't Control

Overthinking often centers on things beyond our control. A powerful mental decluttering technique is to identify and release these thoughts.

Practical Exercise:

1. Draw two circles—one labeled "Control" and the other "No Control."

2. Place each worry in the appropriate circle.

3. Commit to focusing only on the "Control" circle.

"Grant me the serenity to accept the things I cannot change, courage to change the things I can, and wisdom to know the difference." – Reinhold Niebuhr

6.6: Build a Decluttering Routine

Mental decluttering isn't a one-time event—it's an ongoing process. Here's a simple routine to maintain clarity:

1. Start each morning with a brain dump and prioritize your day.

2. End each day by reflecting on accomplishments and releasing unfinished thoughts.

3. Review your "inputs" weekly to ensure they align with your goals.

"Clutter is not just physical stuff. It's old ideas, toxic relationships, and bad habits. Clutter is anything that does not support your better self." – Eleanor Brownn

Conclusion

Decluttering your mind creates space for peace, creativity, and intentional living. By clearing mental clutter, you'll break free from the cycle of overthinking and gain the clarity needed to focus on what truly matters.

Reflection Questions:

1. What mental clutter is currently weighing you down?

2. What steps can you take today to create mental white space?

3. How can you simplify your daily inputs for a clearer mind?

Chapter 7:

Emotional Resilience – Building Inner Strength

Life is unpredictable, and overthinking often stems from our fear of uncertainty. Emotional resilience is the key to navigating life's ups and downs with grace and composure. This chapter explores how to build inner strength, process emotions effectively, and bounce back from challenges stronger than before.

7.1: Understanding Emotional Resilience

Imagine a tree in a storm. The wind bends its branches, but its deep roots keep it grounded. Emotional resilience is like those roots—it doesn't prevent the storm, but it helps you weather it without breaking.

Resilience is the ability to adapt and recover from adversity. It's not about suppressing emotions or pretending everything is fine. Instead, it's about acknowledging your feelings, learning from experiences, and moving forward with renewed strength.

"You may not control all the events that happen to you, but you can decide not to be reduced by them." – Maya Angelou

7.2: The Connection Between Overthinking and Emotional Resilience

Overthinking thrives on emotional vulnerability. When we feel stressed, insecure, or overwhelmed, our minds spiral into worst-case scenarios. Building resilience helps break this cycle by equipping us to handle emotions constructively.

Lila, a young professional, was devastated when she didn't get her dream job. She spent weeks overthinking, wondering what she could have done differently. Eventually, she decided to focus on what she could control. She sought feedback, improved her skills, and landed an even better job six months later.

Her resilience turned a setback into a stepping stone. Without it, she might have stayed stuck in self-doubt and overthinking.

7.3: Steps to Build Emotional Resilience

1. Acknowledge Your Emotions

   Denying or suppressing emotions only amplifies them. Take a moment to sit with your feelings. Ask yourself, *What am I feeling right now, and why?* Naming your emotions reduces their intensity and helps you process them.

2. **Shift Your Focus to What You Can Control**
When you're overwhelmed, make a list of what's within your control versus what isn't. Focus your energy on the controllable, and let go of the rest.

Example:
If you're nervous about an upcoming presentation, you can't control the audience's reactions, but you can prepare thoroughly and practice confidently.

3. **Cultivate Optimism**

Resilient people see setbacks as temporary and solvable. Instead of thinking, *This is the end,* try reframing it as, *This is a challenge I can overcome.*

7.4: Building Emotional Strength Through Practices

Here are practical ways to strengthen your emotional resilience:

1. **Gratitude Journaling**

Every night, write down three things you're grateful for. This practice trains your brain to focus on the positive, even during tough times.

2. **Mindfulness Meditation**

Spend five minutes each day observing your thoughts without judgment. This helps you manage stress and stay present.

3. **Connecting with Others**

Emotional resilience doesn't mean handling everything alone. Lean on friends, family, or support groups to share your feelings and gain perspective.

4. **Learning from Setbacks**

After a difficult experience, reflect on these questions:

- o **What did I learn?**

- o **How can I grow from this?**

- o **What will I do differently next time?**

7.5: Turning Adversity into Growth

Resilient people see challenges as opportunities to grow. This concept is known as post-traumatic growth—the idea that difficult experiences can lead to positive changes.

After losing her job, Maria felt like her world was crumbling. But instead of dwelling on her loss, she used the time to explore her passion for baking. What started as a hobby turned into a successful small business. Maria's resilience transformed a painful setback into a new beginning.

"Adversity doesn't define you—your response to it does".

7.6: Building Resilience in Everyday Life

Resilience isn't built overnight. It's a skill developed through consistent practice.

Daily Habits for Resilience:

- Start your day with affirmations like, "I can handle whatever comes my way."

- Take breaks during stressful moments to reset and recharge.

- Celebrate small victories to remind yourself of your strength.

Conclusion

Emotional resilience is your superpower against overthinking. It doesn't make life's challenges disappear, but it equips you to face them with courage and composure. By building resilience, you can quiet your mind, process emotions effectively, and bounce back from setbacks stronger than ever.

Reflection Questions:

1. What's one challenge you've faced recently, and how did you respond?

2. How can you practice self-compassion the next time you encounter a setback?

3. What steps can you take this week to strengthen your emotional resilience?

Chapter 8:

Embrace Peace – Maintaining a Clear and Focused Mind

After working through strategies to break free from overthinking, the final step is to embrace lasting peace. This chapter focuses on maintaining a clear, focused mind by integrating daily practices for calm, relinquishing control over what you can't change, and celebrating your journey.

8.1: Daily Practices for Ongoing Calm

Overthinking often creeps back in during moments of stress or uncertainty. To prevent this, it's essential to build habits that keep your mind calm and centered every day.

Practical Techniques for Daily Calm:

1. **Mindful Breathing:** Spend 5–10 minutes focusing on your breath. This simple practice anchors your mind to the present moment.

- o **Example: In stressful situations, take five slow, deep breaths to reset your thoughts.**

- o **Famous Quote: "Feelings come and go like clouds in a windy sky. Conscious breathing is my anchor." – Thich Nhat Hanh**

2. **Morning Intentions: Begin your day by setting a positive and realistic intention.**

  - o **Exercise: Write a sentence like, "Today, I will focus on what I can control and release what I can't."**

3. **Gratitude Check-Ins: Reflect on three things you're grateful for every morning or evening. Gratitude shifts your focus from worries to blessings.**

4. **Digital Detox: Allocate time each day to disconnect from technology. Limit exposure to news or social media that triggers overthinking.**

Maria, a teacher, implemented a morning routine combining mindful breathing and gratitude journaling. She found herself less reactive to challenges throughout the day, creating a ripple effect of calm in her classroom and home.

8.2: Letting Go of the Need for Control

One of the biggest drivers of overthinking is the desire to control outcomes. However, true peace comes from accepting that some things are beyond your influence.

Understanding the Control Spectrum:

1. **What You Can Control:** Your thoughts, actions, and reactions.

2. **What You Can't Control:** Other people's opinions, the future, and unexpected events.

"Serenity is not freedom from the storm but peace within it." – *Anonymous*

Techniques for Letting Go:

- **The Serenity Prayer:** Reflect on these words: "Grant me the serenity to accept the things I cannot change, courage to change the things I can, and wisdom to know the difference."

- **Reframing Uncertainty:** View uncertainty as an opportunity for growth and discovery rather than a threat.

Jake, an entrepreneur, struggled with overthinking business risks. After embracing the mindset of focusing only on controllable factors, he discovered greater clarity and confidence in his decisions.

Exercise:
Make a two-column list:

- Column 1: Things you can control.

- Column 2: Things you can't control. Commit to taking action only on items in Column 1.

8.3: Celebrating Your Progress

Acknowledging your progress is a vital part of maintaining a peaceful mind. It reinforces your efforts, boosts confidence, and keeps you motivated to continue on your journey.

Why Celebrating Matters:

Overthinkers often downplay their accomplishments, focusing instead on what's left undone. Celebrating your wins, no matter how small, helps counter this tendency and fosters a sense of fulfillment.

Ways to Celebrate Your Growth:

1. **Reflect on Milestones:** Take time to review where you started and how far you've come.

   o **Example: "Six months ago, I couldn't sleep because of racing thoughts. Now, I can calm my mind with a simple breathing exercise."**

2. **Reward Yourself:** Treat yourself to something meaningful—whether it's a relaxing day off, a favorite meal, or a new book.

3. **Share Your Journey:** Talk to a trusted friend or write about your progress in a journal. Sharing your story can inspire others and deepen your sense of achievement.

Emma, a lifelong overthinker, threw a small celebration after completing a 30-day mindfulness challenge. The simple act of acknowledging her effort gave her the confidence to tackle bigger goals.

"It's not the mountain we conquer, but ourselves." – Sir Edmund Hillary

Conclusion

Embracing peace isn't a one-time achievement; it's a continuous practice. By incorporating daily habits, letting go of what you can't control, and celebrating your wins, you can maintain a clear, focused mind and live more fully in the present.

Reflection Questions:

1. What daily habit can you start today to maintain your sense of calm?

2. What's one thing you need to let go of to find greater peace?

3. How will you celebrate your progress so far?

A Final Word

You've taken a bold step by addressing your overthinking, and you've equipped yourself with the tools to live a more peaceful and fulfilling life. Remember, this is your journey. It's okay to stumble, but never forget how far you've come.

When faced with challenges, remind yourself: You are no longer a prisoner of your thoughts. You are free to think less and live more.

Reflection Questions:

1. What is one habit from this book that you will carry forward every day?

2. How can you share your transformation with someone else who may need it?

3. What will you do today to celebrate this milestone in your journey?

Thank you for allowing me to be part of your journey. Go forward with confidence, clarity, and the belief that you have everything you need to live a life free from overthinking.

Author's Note

Dear Reader,

Thank you for picking up "Think Less, Live More: Break Free from Overthinking." Writing this book has been a deeply personal journey, and it's an honor to share it with you.

Overthinking is something I've battled with myself—moments of doubt, endless analysis, and the weight of overcomplicating even the simplest decisions. It was through my own struggles that I discovered the immense power of letting go, living in the present, and embracing a lighter, more fulfilling approach to life.

This book is not just a guide; it's a conversation between us. I wanted to share what I've learned, not as an expert, but as someone who understands how overwhelming life can feel when we let our minds take over. My hope is that these pages inspire you to find clarity, peace, and freedom from the noise that holds you back.

You may not overcome overthinking in a single day, but every small step you take counts. Be kind to yourself. Celebrate your progress. And remember, the goal isn't perfection—it's a life where your thoughts support your happiness, not hinder it.

Thank you for allowing me to be part of your journey. I am humbled and grateful to walk alongside you as you take these steps toward a more peaceful and joyful life.

With all my heart,
Ashwanee Gupta

Acknowledgements

Writing this book has been an incredibly transformative journey, and I could not have done it without the support and guidance of so many wonderful individuals.

First and foremost, I would like to thank my family for their unwavering love and belief in me. Your constant encouragement reminded me to stay true to my purpose and keep moving forward, even on the toughest days.

To my friends and mentors, thank you for your wisdom, thoughtful insights, and for inspiring me to push beyond my own mental barriers. Your words often served as the seeds of clarity that helped shape this book.

A heartfelt thanks to my readers who are brave enough to confront their struggles with overthinking. You are the reason I embarked on this journey, and I hope these pages serve as a guiding light in your pursuit of a more peaceful, fulfilling life.

Lastly, I am deeply grateful for the life experiences and moments of introspection—both challenging and enlightening—that became the foundation of this book. Each moment reminded me of the power of resilience and the beauty of living in the present.

This book is as much a personal journey as it is a gift to the world, and for that, I am profoundly grateful.

Ashwanee Gupta

Ashwanee Gupta